WHAT DO
FOLLOWERS
EXPECT OF
LEADERS

PATTI HOLMES

WHAT DO
FOLLOWERS
EXPECT OF
LEADERS

Published by:
Holmes Training & Development
PO Box 358
Oxford, OH 45056

Cover design and inside layout: Ad Graphics, Inc.

Printed in the United States of America

Dedication

To my Irish Mother and German Dad
for your love, influence, humor,
and warm smiles –
I am twice blessed.

Contents

Acknowledgments

I am thankful to all of the **followers** who so candidly shared their insights about their leaders and their hopes for improvement, because they truly cared about their organization and its success.

I am grateful to the many **leaders** who, asked themselves, "What do I need to improve upon to make things better for all of us?" for they truly cared about changing themselves in order to strengthen their organization.

A special thanks to **HT & D office staff** through the years; Kris Wilhelm, Ellen Weisman, Beth Newton, and Molly Mack who made it possible for me to do what I believe I am supposed to be doing in life. And to Beth Quick, the person who provides all of the organization and back up to deliver our work with care, special attention and sincerity. You are the solid foundation of our success and I am grateful for your guidance.

A hearty thanks to Di Princell, a dear, loyal, friend of my heart who continues to be the sweet music of morale to my spirit. Thank you to Char Rohr, Anne Whelpton, Joan Bowie and Joan Fox who have always supported my dreams, goals, and my family.

Thanks **Erin**, my lovely and wise daughter, who through the years has become my best friend and teacher. To **Ryan** and **Mattie**, my two boys who I love dearly and have supported my work through their patience and understanding. It is from you three that I have learned the most authentic lessons in life.

And finally, as he inspires me in many ways, **my father** has challenged and continues to call me to be strong in spirit, be filled with laughter and to leave everyone with a smile!

Introduction

This is a book about the true feelings of employees and what they expect from their leaders.

It offers inspiration, as well as, very practical tips from employees who I have surveyed over the past 15 years as a professional speaker and organizational consultant.

Today, many leaders frown at the "soft stuff." Maybe because the soft stuff is the hard stuff to do – this is a book about the right stuff.

My hope is that leaders will use my book as a tool to identify and uncover areas they need to strengthen and then challenge themselves to improve.

Strengthening their relationships with themselves first, then with others, leaders then have the potential to become that person in our lives "who really made a difference."

COMMUNICATE
EFFECTIVELY

*The basic building block
of good communications is the
feeling that every human being
is unique and of value.*

Fred A. Manske Jr.

Please listen to me!
It's the highest
form of respect.

Active listening
takes concentration.

Two ears –
one mouth –
use them wisely!

Look me in the eye.

Never yell
(we lose the message
because we are startled
by the sheer volume
of your voice).

Make connections
for others.

Build a shared understanding
of what we are about in an
organization. It gives meaning
and purpose to our work.

Form trusting relationships.

A dose of sarcasm or words that
hurt are tough to swallow.

Give me immediate feedback
(good or bad).

Ask rather than tell me to help.

Receive my questions
positively – I am then
encouraged to continue
clarifying information.

Periodically, talk about
the issues I raise first.

Make allowances when
personal problems may affect
my office behavior.

Take interest in me
and know that I am not just
a tool for your success.

Cultivate mutual respect.

*Ask me what's wrong
with customer service.*

Be compassionate and
understanding.

Answer
all questions.

Express yourself
with conviction.

Walk in my
shoes.

Don't be embarrassed
by your emotions.

Discipline yourself to
always have a friendly
and outgoing nature.

Let us see that you have
a sense of humor.

Ask how I am feeling
after being off for a sick day.

Praise me in public and
correct me in private.

***Please know that your way
may not be the best way
or the only way.***

Respect my
confidences.

Ask me how
I want to be rewarded.

Call me by name.

Ask me good questions.

Interrupt me –
only with applause.

Communicate up, down,
across and around (the grapevine
is not the most effective way).

Don't contribute
to gossip.

Inquire about
my family.

Let me share my ideas
with you on the
organization's mission.

Write me a handwritten
note to say thanks.

Know my birthday,
and at least acknowledge
it verbally.

Keep me informed directly
whenever possible.

Ask me how my weekend
was and then listen
to my response.

Let us know if you are selling
the company before the news
hits the streets.

Tell me how I fit into the
entire organizational structure.

Be friendly and approachable.

Be available when
I need advice, assistance or
additional information.

Avoid putting your desk
between you and me.

Continue to truly
influence and inspire me.

Be in touch.

Mean what you say and
say what you mean.

Speak up!

*Be aware of the power
of your non-verbal
communication.*

Don't flirt.

If you see I am hurting,
ask me about it.

Be the best listener
in the entire organization.

*Don't close your eyes
and look the other way.
Demand and encourage
high standards.*

Hold people's
feet to the fire!

Ask me how *I* think
things are going.

Refrain from talking
negatively about other
employees to me – if you do,
I know you're talking
about me too.

Read my body language –
it is more powerful than
the spoken word.

Have an open door policy –
but not without an open heart.

Please don't finish
my sentences.

Keep us informed of the
financial stability of
the company.

*On occasion, ask us
who is truly competent
around here – we know.*

Addressing the entire
organization as a group
is crucial – we want to
hear from you.

Know my first and last name
and how to pronounce
it correctly.

Don't say "I'll get back to
you on that" when you
know you won't!

Build relationships,
not structure.

Be clear, specific, and to the
point in your directions to me.

*Operate with substance,
not style.*

Respect me enough
to tell me the truth.

Manage by walking around (MBW) instead of managing by fear (MBF).

Create resonance with me not dissonance, so I may speak with you openly and work with you easily.

When you address the
employees, show your respect
by rehearsing your presentation.
Anticipate questions and
challenge us with your message.

*Be consumed with character,
not personality.*

CREATE A POSITIVE ENVIRONMENT

Nothing is more important than creating an environment in which people feel they make a difference. You can't feel good about what you're doing unless you think you're making a difference.

Jack Stack

Know your people.

Familiarize us with
the workflow patterns
as quickly as possible.

Begin and finish meetings
on time.

Keep the employee
manual current.

We're not a Mom and Pop
organization anymore –
let's grow up.

*Give me my performance
appraisals on time, every time,
and let us also evaluate you.*

Instill in everyone that
they are the organization.

Let the employees plan the
annual holiday party, summer
picnics, or annual banquet.

Ask me to be on an employee
team – then ask me to lead
an employee team.

Never tolerate
sexual harassment.

If you are committed to
customer service, don't forget
your *employees* are your most
important customers.

Deal with direction not speed.

Let me be involved in the
decision making process.

Improve my physical
working conditions.

Inform me ahead of time
that my meeting will be delayed.

Don't make hasty decisions.
Have all the facts and
information first.

Don't ask me to do something
for you and then completely
re-do it.

Before policy/procedure
changes are made, think them
through carefully.

Help me to
discover the truth.

*Once a year, have us fill out an
employee satisfaction survey.
Feed the results back to us and
let's develop an action plan to
strengthen our weaknesses.*

Safeguard the environment.

Be willing to take an
unpopular position.

Don't give the
store away.

Build group cohesiveness
and pride.

Be visible.

Be courageous.

*Help me understand
how my individual purpose
can be realized in our
organization.*

Be happy for me when I go
on to bigger and better things.
I only grew because of your
investment in me.

*Shape our culture to
support excellence.*

Trust my competency and
my judgment.

Move us forward with
confidence and clarity.

Encourage freedom of self-
expression – an environment
where it's OK to "talk back."

Make this place more FUN.

Anticipate, be open and
eager to change.

Assure that the workplace
environment is safe and clean.

Give me challenging and
meaningful work assignments.

Keep staff meetings organized;
have a written agenda; be brief
and to the point; hold all
members responsible for
preparation and participation;
record all action items.

Meet me in my office area
or work space instead of
always in your office.

Let me know where I can reach you in the event of an emergency, and let me know when you'll be returning.

Minimize surprises ten minutes before closing the office.

Could we sincerely work at being proactive instead of constantly reactive?

Don't play favorites just
because of personality, looks,
attire or personal demeanor.

Don't light up the
office by leaving it!

Don't use your position
to interrupt the normal flow
of work – respect the chain
of command.

Have an accessible and workable succession plan in place.

Avoid making "guest appearances" at the office – have a true presence.

Don't believe or accept everything from the person who has "your ear!"

Only hire competent family members who have had three years of experience with another organization, and don't give them any special treatment.

Learn from the custodian ... they often have the best insight of all.

Help us understand change, everyone wants to grow but not everyone likes to change.

Make sure everyone pulls
their own weight.

Ask if there is anything
we can do better.

Don't just give lip service to
total quality, strategic planning,
or empowerment; do it right or
don't do it at all.

Focus on the business at hand.

Please be there for me
even when I screw up.

Realize that I learn more
from my failures than from my
successes. Create and support
an environment that makes
it okay to make a mistake
as long as we learn from it!

Create a library of resource
materials in our organization
for me to grow both personally
and professionally.

Give power away – you then
become more powerful.

Make sure the person
who evaluates me knows what
I do and the true quality
of my work.

Get rid of dead weight.

Don't adopt AFP (another fine program) or POTM (program of the month) unless you are truly committed to having it be the very best it can be over the long haul.

Celebrate our accomplishments.

Articulate our values – it's important to gain agreement on how to demonstrate our shared values and hold people accountable.

Don't microwave everything we do. Sometimes we need a crock pot.

One day could I have an office with a window?

Allow "us" to evaluate
our supervisors and listen
to what we say.

If you are leading the sales team,
make sure processes are in place
to cook all that you kill.

You know where you are going.
God knows where you are going.
But do I know where you
are going?

MODEL
THE WAY

The character of an organization is established by the character of the people who work there. And that character is determined by the integrity of the leader.

Robert Rosen

Model the behavior
you want from me.

Please admit your own
mistakes. I like knowing
you are human too.

Create an environment where
people are open to receiving
advice or constructive criticism.

Keep current in
our profession.

Walk, talk, breathe, and live
quality and excellence.

*Do what you say
you are going to do.*

Enter the workplace
each day cheerfully setting
a positive tone.

Always operate with honor.

Be a servant of the people.

Set our direction.

Be authentic.

Employees want a model
not a motto!

Always be prepared.

Treat your spouse with
the utmost respect.

Be the finest team member.

Be consistent in your
temperament.

Make tough decisions and
never look back.

If you are going to model
the way, you have to
understand the way.

Be credible.

Lead the shift from
position power to people power.

If you can't be charismatic, just give us your very best smile.

Call all of us to be leaders.

Operate with integrity.

Be a respected contributing
member of the community.

Be trustworthy.

Know your stuff.

Make sure your actions and
your words always match.

*Identify what we stand for
and then demonstrate it daily.*

Be on time.

Confirm what you say in writing;
keep good documentation.

Don't be the loudest voice –
don't be the softest voice.

Be supportive, encouraging,
and kind.

I expect you to be in charge –
so lead me with strength –
I want to follow you.

Be energetic,
upbeat and fun!

Challenge the process when
you believe you are right.

Be the last to leave one
company social each year.

Continue to be involved in
leadership groups, chamber
activities and professional
associations. Your always being
a student brings newness and
energy to our organization.

Take risks.

Don't be grouchy!

Be the same person inside
these walls as you are outside
these walls.

Don't engage in sexist or ethnic
comments or jokes.

Continue to support the arts
in our community.

*When you support
in-house skills training,
stay for the session yourself,
not just the introduction.*

Take your turn on the
customer service lines.

Show us a balance between
work and family.

I expect you to be
perfectly imperfect.

Always tell the truth.

Be fair.

Know and act on the principle
"that the person closest
to the job has the best
information about the job."

Be consistent.

Be a river, not a rock –
flexibility is crucial.

Read current leadership
materials, good books, and
articles and share with all of us.

Wear a holiday tie or
pin – show spirit.

*Devote as much
energy and time to our
organization as you do
to your golf game.*

STRENGTHEN PERSONAL SKILLS

*In the end, it is important
to remember that we cannot
become what we need to be by
remaining what we are.*

Max DePree

Like yourself – have
positive self-regard.

Know your own
weaknesses and shortcomings –
we already know them.

*Develop yourself to
your highest potential.*

Understand and practice
emotional intelligence –
for when you operate with
positive emotions the entire
organization benefits.

Have your leadership style
assessed and share the results.

Take a break when
you are stressed.

Even though you think
you have arrived, you haven't.
Be a life-long learner.

Go home to your family.

Admitting your mistakes
contributes to your strengths.
Covering up contributes
to your weaknesses.

Be considerate,
caring and courteous.
(People don't *care* how much
you *know* until they *know*
how much you *care*.)

Be respectful.

Loosen up!
Life is too short to
always be uptight.

Disagree without
being disagreeable.

Remember your roots!

Use your time wisely, as many
of us want your attention.

Eat lunch with me
sometimes, and don't forget
to treat occasionally.

Let me know of
your family.

Exude enthusiasm and
optimism – your attitude
is contagious.

Remember to send
flowers or a card to me in the
hospital and if appropriate you
can come and visit me.

Ask my opinion.

Recognize, appreciate,
and respect the differences
between men and women.

Laugh with me.

Look at everything.
"Staple yourself to an order."

Be sensitive to my need
for individual recognition.

Respect my background
and traditions.

Introduce yourself to
my family and children.

Come to my loved one's funeral.

Send me a card or call me
when I'm sick.

Be sensitive.

Be graceful.

Don't lose your temper –
always be cool (A.B.C.).

Keep physically fit and
mentally strong. Be neat
and dress professionally.

Take time to contemplate.

Strengthen your spirit.

Devote time for
personal renewal.

Don't miss the moment.

Read!

Believe in who you are and
what you are doing.

Remember what you did
right in the beginning that
made you successful.

Keep my confidences.

Value me every day – not just
at the Holiday Party or
Annual Awards Banquet.

Let us know what you
care about most.

Tell us who made a difference
in your life and why.

Share the history of
the organization.

Leave a legacy.

INSPIRE AND MOTIVATE

Our core values, mission, and vision have to come down off of the wall, jump out of the frame and into our hearts and put a new beat in our step.

Patti Holmes

Don't give me a turkey for Thanksgiving, if you treat me like a lame duck all year.

Occasionally, buy me a Pepsi – graciously and willingly.

Invest in my personal and professional development – send me off to a seminar or workshop as a perk.

Encourage cross-training
opportunities with me.

Discuss with me my future
within the organization.

Continually support
Employee Assistance Programs.

Encourage, demonstrate and
support a deep commitment
to family.

Be visionary. I want to know
where you want to go, and
inspire me to go with you.

Keep "Breakfast with
the Boss" going. They're great
informal sessions and people
are opening up.

Please recognize me when
I go the distance.

Share success in creative ways –
such as stock options
or ownership.

Have a five-year strategic
plan that you share and are
dedicated to – I want to buy into
that plan so we work together
and complement one another.

Invest in me – I'm your most important asset.

Give me the big picture; where do I fit in, what are your plans for me – what is my future with you?

Create loyalty with me
and make me want to run
through walls for you.

Be creative in rewards and
recognition. There are many
other ways to value me other
than my paycheck.

Let me know you believe
in something and have faith.

*Take me to a better place,
I want to go with you.*

Instill in us a
sense of urgency.

Conduct meetings to determine our shared values. Then follow up with discussions on how we demonstrate behavior that supports our values.

Give me important work to do.

Be the most positive person in our organization.

Make heroes of your employees through visibility and recognition.

See the good in people.

Take responsibility for your attitude. It takes no responsibility to be negative but incredible discipline to be positive.

Appeal to our emotions.

Show a deep belief in me.

Don't be critical –
be analytical.

Give recognition and credit
when deserved and in a
timely fashion.

Pull me along – don't push me.

If you want to know how
to reward me – ask me,
I'll tell you.

Motivate me
through persuasion.

Celebrate our
accomplishments.

CARE.

Develop your people –
it's your most important
responsibility.

Delegate –
follow-up – and then
delegate again.

Reward creativity;
creative ideas keep employees
and the business alive.

Give me credit
for my ideas.

Focus on individual
productivity, not potential.

Please spend time,
money and energy on
training and development.

Lead our organization
in commitment to giving
back to the community.
Encourage me to be involved.

BE A MASTER TEACHER

*What make greatness
is starting something that
lives after you.*

Ralph W. Sockman

Don't play favorites.

Criticize respectfully.
Don't point a finger and
assign blame.

Concentrate on fixing
the system and making it better.
Remember to ask, "How can we
improve the situation and what
can I do to help?"

Include me in decisions
that will affect me. Then I will
have ownership and will
follow through.

Discipline to the system
and not to the individual
whenever possible.

Be fair.

Demonstrate confidence
in my abilities.

Respect differences.

Don't take issue with my feelings.
Instead show compassion and
validate my feelings because then
you validate me.

Teach me about goal setting and let me know you are willing to help me reach my goals.

Encourage me to read motivational and inspirational materials.

Support my involvement in professional activities and associations.

Give me an opportunity to lead.

Be a positive agent
for change.

Encourage me to lead a meeting
or give a presentation.

Empower me. I need responsibility plus authority, sufficient knowledge and skill, adequate and timely information and high self-confidence and esteem to be truly successful.

Let me go!

Let me represent you at a meeting or function.

Give me boundaries and then
coach me to stay within them.

Lead from the inside out.

*I want to see your spirit,
your strength, and your soul.*

Make intelligent choices
with input from us.

Recognize and appreciate
my ideas.

*Allow me to take risks and
make mistakes. We learn more
from our mistakes than any
of our successes.*

Show trust in my ability
to know my work area, and
trust in my ability to make
the best decisions that affect
that work area.

Emphasize fairness, firmness
and accountability.

*Be prepared with
conscious planning.*

Trust me to do my work; don't
keep looking over my shoulder.

Don't ever let me get
too comfortable – when I'm
comfy, my quality slips.

Instill pride!

Enrich the lives of others.

Encourage me to change.
Our past is not our potential.

Provide me with a
job description that is clear.
Then my performance evaluation
will be much easier to accomplish
and more beneficial to both of us.

Have a deep appreciation for
people's differences.

*Don't expect me to be really
good at a task if no one has
taken the time to teach me
how to do it right.*

Keep a performance diary
so when you evaluate me, the
evaluation adequately reflects my
overall performance and not just
the past 30 days.

Expect the best from me
and then you'll get it.

Strengthen people through
information; no information,
no responsibility, no ownership,
no caring, no involvement,
no commitment.

Maintain our
high standards.

*Value individual and group
differences – we are better
because of the strength of
our diversity.*

Teach us how to set goals
and acknowledge us when
we achieve them.

Let me have input into the tools and resources to do my job.

Stretch me. I'm capable of more than you think.

Don't just give me responsibility; give me authority too.

Post and share your favorite
quotes with all of us.

Explain to me why we do
things the way we do.

Develop yourself to your
highest potential

Adversity makes us dig deep –
show us the way.

*Make a difference
in my life.*

For more information about Patti Holmes'
speaking engagements, consulting, workshops,
books and cassette tapes, write or call:

Patti Holmes
Holmes Training & Development
PO Box 358
Oxford, OH 45056
513-523-1394
513-893-3602 (fax)

www.pattiholmes.com

Patti's most requested programs:

Building an Attitude of Excellence
The Spirit of Leadership
Would You Work for You?
Utilizing Your Strength in Sales
Valuing One Another in the Workplace
The Ethical Manager
Celebrating Your Organization's Success

Enriching, Educating and Energizing
Individuals and Organizations Since 1988.